Wakefield Press

smoke

Miriel Lenore is an Adelaide poet who has worked as a plant breeder, a student counsellor and teacher. After twenty-two years in Fiji, she returned to Australia and began a women's study course in 1984. There she wrote her first published poem.

Miriel's interest in studying women's lives and the interaction of people and places has resulted in the wide-ranging subjects of her books, from the explorer Edward John Eyre to botanic gardens and a Western Desert community. Most recently she has researched the lives of three of her nineteenth-century grandmothers.

Now a grandmother herself, in *Smoke* Miriel Lenore looks back at the experiences of the girl who lived in a small town on the edge of the Mallee, surrounded by three lakes and a hill.

Also by Miriel Lenore

Poetry
the Lilac Mountain
sun wind & diesel
travelling alone together:
in the footsteps of Edward John Eyre
drums & bonnets
the Dog Rock
in the garden
a wild kind of tune

Performance
Text of *Masterkey*
with Mary Moore
(who adapted the novel by Masako Togawa)

smoke

Wakefield Press

Miriel Lenore

Wakefield Press
16 Rose Street
Mile End
South Australia 5031
www.wakefieldpress.com.au

First published 2019

Cover designed by Liz Nicholson, Wakefield Press
Text designed and typeset by Clinton Ellicott, Wakefield Press

ISBN 978 1 74305 644 8

A catalogue record for this
book is available from the
National Library of Australia

Wakefield Press thanks
Coriole Vineyards for
continued support

for Brian, my brother

companionably silent
my brother and I pick mushrooms
on the hills behind his house

buckets full
we lean on opposite sides
of the ute

tell me he says
do you remember our childhood
as terribly unhappy?

happy you mean?
unhappy I mean

together   alone
we drive back
to mushrooms on toast

contents

. . . three lakes and a hill

Australia Felix

i
'A land so inviting
        and still without inhabitants'
explorer Mitchell said of the rich Loddon Plains

the inhabitants he couldn't see
        yet described as 'fine and friendly'
were soon to be driven off
      or killed by the diseases my tribe brought
as they rushed stock into a land
        so swiftly made infelicitous

within ninety years blown sand buried fences
        covered the new ones built on top
dust storms darkened the daylight
        carried topsoil to the sea
plates on kitchen tables of abandoned farms

ii
not all the newcomers left –
        with better methods   other crops
my home town and its neighbours flourished
lucerne   tomatoes   olives now thrive
        in billiard table paddocks of Loddon water

and the Dja Dja Wurrung I never saw as a child
are here
      defending their culture in court
a main street memorial honours
        the ancestors who never left

the river

big enough to be on school maps   the Loddon
        snakes through Dja Dja Wurrung country
small now   its strength left
            in the dams near its source
buttressed by red gums   high banks remain
        it's a brown god: the Ancient of Days

this is our boundary — we leave for the big shops
        beach holidays   family visits   horse races
the Agricultural Shows

once we cross the rickety bridge on return
we're in familiar territory   the road curving
            past lignum at Yando turnoff
the river flats at Fyfes
the Mysia signpost near Boort's first township
and the ancient camps of the Yung Balug clan

after the pioneer station with its lonely graves
we cruise up the rise
            to our returning view of home
curled between lunette and the lake
            filled by the life-giving Loddon

smoke

Boort my home town: three lakes and a hill
        swamps north and south
mallee to the west   black box to the east
     where the River Loddon roams

Boort and sold my friends laugh
I tell them *boort* is smoke to the Dja Dja Wurrung
    as in signals from the hill
as in hearth as in destruction in every culture

I was born at Nurse Morrison's beside the Little Lake
and unlike the first babies was not carefully smoked
for health and holiness but cleansed against germs
     in nurse's old enamel bowl

the dining room fireplace in our first home
belched smoke over card games at change of wind
and wispy clouds from my father's cigarettes
     foreshadowed his far-off painful death

. . . a patch of dress

first memory

thrilled and scared
I'm flying to the ceiling
then caught in my father's
              big hands
up again and again

stop it Bill
        it's dangerous
a pattern for these new parents
        as they learn on me

Eva Caroline

my mother shared small Salvation Army houses
        with her parents   three sisters   five brothers
moving most years to a new town   new school

Eve never fitted into Army ways:
        she crept out to forbidden films
                        crawled under circus tents
stole her sister's chocolates
                        replacing them with stones
hated tambourines and drums in the street

her eldest sister wrote home:
        I hope she has got out of the way
        of going to the WC during the washing up
brave enough though to rescue
        two drowning children from the river

        Teachers' College was her paradise –
dancing each night for warmth before study
        choosing amusing boyfriends over serious
savouring new ideas   new ways of teaching
        friendships begun here lasted a lifetime
and college songs became our lullabies

        a bit flighty she said of her younger self
laughed to tell of local lads at her first teaching post
hauling her on the mattress from her hotel room
        into the main street   and leaving her

Cyril Sydney

my father was thirteen pounds at birth:
his poor mother   her fourth and last child
    Cyril to her   Sid to his father
    Bill to his siblings

asked aged four what he wanted to be
he didn't hesitate:
        a bullock driver
          why?
        so I can swear

early he learnt to run into the back hut
at sound of their raucous father in the street
his sister's crossed fingers
             meant silence
until his mother locked the knives away

pampered by sisters Doris and Ethel
    he followed his older brother
        into mischief
though he preferred horses to Hal's guns

his siblings left home to study or teach
    Bill had to stay   relinquishing
the Melbourne scholarship he won –
        no money for his keep
farmhand at 13   up at four harnessing the horses
        his wages paid the grocer

at twenty he coaxed the farmer into sharing
    a business as agents and carters
mimic and spinner of yarns
    Bill sang in the church choir
            if he liked the minister

good at sport – billiards   cricket   tennis
football too
    until a famous Yando-Appin game
when he   his friend Les   and the Appin captain
    scored broken bones and bans for life

destiny

grey-green eyes   stylish clothes
wavy hair bobbed in the twenties' style
Eve is off to her first permanent posting:
Infant Mistress   Boort State School
the Headmaster has offered to find board

three trains in 170 miles from Melbourne
she shares space with a tired woman
whose two unruly sons scuffle on the floor –
Eve's stern teacher look has no effect
she moves her smart new shoes out of range

the carriage empties at Boort
the Headmaster is at the station
drives her to a large weatherboard house
with rambling garden and two tall palms
introduces her landlady
yes   it is the mother of those tiresome boys
Eve eats a chocolate ginger in her room

that night she meets a tall young man
she takes to be the farmhand
later finds he's the landlord's business partner
later still   she marries him

Sans Souci

standing in the circle of his arms
her head reaches his ear as he bends
she smiles at the camera
                     giving nothing away
he smiles down at her   protective   proud

teaching or marriage?
          she knows she can't have both
uncertain   she moves to another town
                     another school
after a year decides for Bill and Boort
          with one condition:

she would never live on a farm
                               with cows to milk
hens horses dogs and shearers to feed
          Bill the businessman agrees

no formal photo of my parents' wedding exists
          only a snapshot as they leave the church
a woman and hat come between
                     camera and bride
my mother is represented by an elegant leg
          a fashionable shoe
and a patch of dress I'm told was green

they build a weatherboard and fibro house
in Kiniry Estate where the butter factory
                     chugs night and day
making electricity   ice   butter

they call the house SANS SOUCI
– happy-go-lucky – they are and hope to be
plan a stained glass panel with the name

when installed in the front door
        it reads SANS SAUCI
they laugh and keep it

. . . the world is chancy

bon appétit

from my high chair
I'm protesting
    at mashed vegies
my mother
    spoons the mush
with an incantation:
    one for Auntie Elsie
    one for Auntie Grace
    through dozens of
    unknown relatives:
genealogy
ingested with the greens

marked for life

my mother blames my father
for the scar on my thigh –
a careless cigarette burn
he denies   she insists

I'm sure the mark came
later from loose iron
in a friend's woolshed
my father innocent

I gained my second blemish
the scar on my forehead
when I jiggled my playpen
off the veranda and fell on a brick
no parent at fault   all's well

child

in my sixty-sixth year I wake
    with my heart falling out
hear myself scream for mother

surrounded by love   yet I call for her
    as from my old bedroom
where the demons crept
    through the quince tree
        and in the window

mostly she kept them at bay
    with each evening's ritual
first the reading of stories:
    Blinky Bill   the Pooh books
and my favourite Wind in the Willows

College songs followed:
    Gaudeamus igitur
    Eton Boating Song
    the Teachers' College anthem

gliding from my bed
    Mum danced from the room
waving back as she sang
    Goodnight Ladies
    I'm going to leave you now
when the door shut   life ended

the Furphy cart

was I five or four?
deserted for a funeral interstate
(you took my baby brother though)
    left with friends I didn't know
    on a farm I'd never seen

sleeping alone in a fly-wire annexe
ghosts owls and a she-oak sighing
    I lay wide-eyed in darkness
ready to speed at first light
        to the kitchen fire
safe for another day

behind a shed
    I found a Furphy water cart
embossed with writing I could read:
    good better best
    never let it rest
    till your good is better
    and your better best

I knew you'd want me brave and good
    not snivelling to 'Auntie' Jean
I whispered those Furphy words each night
    until you rescued me

Infant Room lessons

vivid in the morning sun
red geraniums on the window sill
taught me Left from Right
    as I faced the King's picture

I learnt to worship sitting at the feet
    of glorious Miss Freda Edwards
as she pointed to pictures
    of Aapples Bballs and Ccats
carefully drawn in coloured chalk
    on the blackboard

when I copied other kids in Grade 1
    by carving my initials into the desk
Miss Pedler loomed over me:
    I expected better of you Miriel
a refrain that dogged me through much of life

seated near the geraniums in Grade 2
I saw our trainee Miss Sutherland drop and die
    in front of us
she lay motionless until Mr Pryor from Grade 6
    carried her away

she returned next day
    her fainting fit teaching me
    that the world is chancy

watermelon

we peered through the cumbungi
edging our swimming hole
at thatched huts in market gardens
men in conical straw hats
the nearest we came to *the foreign*

one hot summer day
I went with my father on business
to Louey and his brothers
in their low windowless home
thatched like a stable

Dad said their money went to China
none left for a house like ours
and no wives to tidy or complain
I peeked uncertainly into dark corners

while the men smoked and yarned
I pictured myself in China with dragons
sat on the dirt floor composing stories
trying to ignore the dark behind me

as we left Louey gave me a slice
of cooling watermelon   put his hand
on my fair hair and called me Silver
               I had a friend

Thor's voice

I knew nothing of thunder gods
      yet grew up terrified of storms
didn't know what caused
      the sound or the light
all I knew was you mustn't stand near trees
      or carry metal
and if you counted to three
      between flash and crash
      you were still alive

do I believe in foetal imprinting?
      when pregnant with me
my mother looked from the window in a storm
      to see the paperboy struck by lightning
and carried onto our veranda to die

six years later I ran home from school in panic
      as a storm came in from the west
a small metal name tag on my schoolbag
      would surely attract the lightning
Truscotts' gate was open   I rushed to hide my bag
      under their big cypress hedge
freed from the dangerous metal   I raced home
      to collapse into safety

the scientist

outside the bedroom   Sunny South roses
        inside   the dressing table is a mess
the embroidered cover hangs over the edge
crystal powder-bowl perilously close
        hairbrush and comb set fallen

the toddler Brian
                sunlit in his uniform of red
sits entranced
                in a litter of wheels and cogs
fingering the black roman numerals
        on the face of our mother's gold watch

Brian doesn't hear her enter
                or the stifled groan
doesn't see her tightened jaw as she pours
        into a jar the tiny brass pieces
the remains of her parents'
        twenty-first birthday gift

she lifts the boy onto her hip
        carefully closes the door behind her –
perhaps Mr Halfhide in his cluttered shop
                can work a miracle
but this is the Depression
        the watch never leaves the jar

the journey

my parents growl at me
I don't deserve it   it's not fair
I'll go away   they'll be sorry

I march to my room   fill a bag with clothes
and my koala companion Blinky Bill
stomp through the kitchen
        I'm leaving

the monsters don't even look
Dad reading   Mum tidying up
        oh goodbye then
        safe travels

I'm shocked   why aren't they worried?
mean and heartless
they'll miss me when I'm gone

at the front gate   which way?
across the road to Marshalls?
but Mrs Marshall will bring me back

Mr Jackson? he has a grumbly voice
no kids in the street   no one to tell
it's getting dark

slowly I open the kitchen door
the monsters look up
        welcome home
        want some cocoa?

to see the Duke

Annie Lewis is taking her nephews
  invites me to come
up early dressed warmly
we are ready for the rail motor at 9

the Duke of Gloucester the King's son
is coming to Korong Vale 17 miles away
I've seen his photo –
all gold braid ropes and ribbons
  and a furry hat with a feather

arriving Annie adds more nephews
to her flock before we walk to the oval
join children from nearby towns
  standing in rows behind the rails

we wait
    and wait
      and wait

we fidget as the wind gets up
    but the sun is smiling –
the Duke's gold should still gleam

he's coming!
a shiny black car hood down
    drives onto the arena
a man in a fawn overcoat stands in the back
  his arm half lifted in a slow wave
his hat is the same as my dad's

saltbush hedge

the only indigenous plant in our garden
the same in all seasons   part of the land

roses and cypress along most fences
for us the grey survivor of the inland

exemplary as a catcher of dust
from the gravel path and road

thick   untidy   matted until Dad
finds time to trim this fortress

silver leaves gradually turn rusty
until winter rain washes them clean

solid backdrop for family photos
sensible but impossible to love

yet when I return years later
the house looks naked without it

dripping wet

behind the saltbush hedge
I ride my tricycle around the lawn
my mother weeds the rose bed

the gate squeaks open
young Brian stumbles up the path
dripping wet and crying:

I called and you didn't come
anger and relief collide in Mum's voice:
        why did . . . where were?

she gathers him in her arms
bundles him inside to dry –
he'd wandered   fallen into the channel

I sit on the front step
knowing Mum will shake her head
repeat this story with exasperated pride

so this is how envy feels
I'm learning that good girls never attain
the starring roles of wayward boys

shape

with a hairbrush Mum taps
    my front teeth straight
tries to curl my hair in rags
makes me gargle Condy's
    crystals against diphtheria
teaches me to read and write
carefully moving the pencll
      to my right hand

Dad brings back fish from the river
shows me felted goldfinch nests
and the spectacular
     rainbow bird
teaches me to drive ride and shoot
merely regretting that I can't cook
or 'entertain a drawing room'

only at tennis do they unite
to coach and cheer   proud
when I captain the team
    or win a clock

fame

Kelvin Rodgers swallowed a six-inch nail!
the news darts around the schoolyard
kids playing chasey pause
even those at the marbles ring stop
how big is a six-inch nail?   he's just three
how could the nail go down?

two operations in Melbourne fail:
he must go to Philadelphia
to Professor Chevalier Jackson's care
Kelvin and his mum will travel by ship
thanks to funds raised despite the Depression

newspapers from Perth to Townsville
follow the boy with the nail in his lung:
1½ inches long with a half-inch head
its size varies in the papers: 3 inches in Sydney
11 in Launceston   14 in Perth

in seven minutes the miracle nail is retrieved
Kelvin returns in triumph   a star on the ship
dressed in a special sailor suit
he steers the ship through Sydney Heads

the grandfather cup

Fernihurst Weir   Marmal   Lake Meran
carnivals are high points of our year –
New Year's Day   Australia Day   Easter
        the whole district comes
for cordials and icecream from a churn
we compete at tennis and races
        swims and swings are for fun
I envy young lovers in shining innocence
        paired off to play Drop the Hanky

I'm fascinated with the Wheel of Fortune
watch as it spins and stops
the box of chocolates changes hands
        I long to risk my shilling
stand there   too cautious   too shy

when Eileen Mills at the Yando Festival
        won a grandfather cup
ledged at the rim for a huge moustache
she gave it to my clean-shaven father
        'to look after'

the cup sat in a cupboard forgotten
until one day I spied it
        played with it   broke it
saw Mum's father   newly dead   glare at me
        from heaven above the cupboard

Nellie Beattie

outside the familiar streets of town
alone among the saltbush and gypsum flats
your tiny cottage held   I'm sure   a cat

Mondays as you waddled past the window
to do our weekly wash   Brian and I –
thrilled and scared in our wickedness –
changed a nursery song about a beetle:
> *Miss Beattie kept a shoe shop*
> *inside a hollow oak*

you judged jams and pickles
at our local Show   were also
the authority on cheese and ham

we came to you when valuables
were lost like Janet's engagement ring
bought after Tommy's horse had won

look in the chook yard by the nest
and there it was
behind your back   we murmured *witch*

liniment and roses

smallest room in the house   our bathroom
prison for the naughty
        razor strop hung on the door   a warning
chip heater   bath with shower   basin   linen press
barely room to turn around   busy on Saturdays

useful in heat waves   all day we dipped
in the half-filled bath   relief after sweating
        in the hall – the coolest place

in winter the heater roared after home matches
        as footballers covered in mud and blood
cleaned their wounds for the return to district farms
        the liniment remained in the air for days

one glorious night of the annual tennis tournament
        the room was again a traffic hub
the beautiful people from Melbourne stayed on a farm
but used our homely bathroom after the game
        to prepare for The Ball

coming in cream flannels and skirts
        they transformed into gowned princesses
        or penguin-suited princes
lavender and attar of roses filled the air

our parents too
        were part of the miracle
for us danced the Charleston down the passage
we watched starry eyed   no need for dreams
        our fairytale world was here

holiday

our family is off to Sydney by car
    first stop   relatives in Shepparton
we load empty biscuit tins for return to the factory
(Auntie Madge is an Arnott –
             they get them free)
next day the tins clatter from the luggage rack
            onto the highway
Dad reclaims and secures them more carefully

with the Murrumbidgee flooded below Gundagai
    we detour to Mum's cousin
stay in strange rooms with patterned tin ceilings

driving through Bradman's town
    we're into the real world of important
        people and places
uncles and aunts will take us to Manly
    Dee Why   The Bridge   Taronga Zoo

visiting Mum's wealthy uncle I'm scared –
he shows us the cane he'll use if we're naughty
    I believe him
he owns the house
    where D.H. Lawrence wrote *Kangaroo*
the family verdict:
'terrible man   backyard a disgrace   rubbish everywhere'

the Big Lake

aided by a tyre tube
        I learn to swim with the yabbies
      in the channel between Big and Little Lakes
soon graduate to a corner of the Big Lake
           skirted by cumbungi: --
our swimming hole
      defined by a floating platform
our club rooms   two benches
     and two change sheds of corrugated iron
         open to the sky
nail holes in the girls' shed allow boys to peep

    I have two photos taken at the Lake
in the first I'm at Margaret Bowman's
        fourth birthday party
we're in a small play tent under the river red gums
        just two of us
we sit with her present   a tin of toffees between us
the sun sets over the water
       a golden pathway to our canvas cave
this is a good party   I hope she'll open the toffees

    in the second photo I'm nine
our family has been swimming
       hair tousled and wet
I'm in green overalls my mother made   Brian is too
Dad is putting his border collie through his tricks
     jumping over a stick held higher and higher
dog and man filled with pride
        we kids enthralled
Mum smiling distantly   immaculate
      and almost out of the picture

the Bank

an easy drop-off point close to Melbourne
the National Bank was our holiday home
where Auntie Dod seemed to exist
only to ensure our happiness
we hardly knew Uncle Jack – a taciturn banker
gardener and cleaner of shoes

their home at the back of the Bank was a palace:
here were girls to play with
(on our street were only boys)
endless rooms to play in
Monopoly could be left unfinished for days
best of all were the Bank rooms
after hours   we could be tellers
counting money
or managers stamping papers

we loved Auntie Dod's warm embraces
after a fall or sleepwalking adventures
or for no reason at all
Brian bought his favourite for her birthday –
a tin of condensed milk

such a surprise then to discover that
in this haven
Uncle Jack slept with a revolver under his pillow

my exotic aunt

I seldom saw Dad's sister Ethel
though she taught in a Melbourne school
    sent good books for my birthday
and postcards from distant places:
Buckingham Palace guards
    and the clock at Wells Cathedral
where on the hour tiny knights appeared for battle
the cards lived in a special tin
    with certificates from my Ginger Meggs Club

Auntie Et went to England to hunt for our ancestors
and Mum told me she had taught in Tonga
    before I knew where Tonga was

the bright one   the risk taker   poor judge of men
    was the family view
known for her charities –
    several Oxfam bulls in Indian villages
sport the name of her beleaguered golf club
I knew she assisted many overseas children
    visited them   left them money in her will

only after her death   I learnt of the single mum
hiding her daughter
    from the Education Department
after four years   it proved impossible
    family friends adopted her 'little flower'
        with one condition:
that she never meet or contact the child again

the game

away from the dozing houses
at the top end of our street
the boys play a risky game

a boy curls into an upright car tyre
with inner tube removed
balances himself with hands held inside

another boy launches the tyre
to whirl down the hill   wobble
and fall over as the track levels

afraid   yet hoping to belong
I ask for a turn   *you'll have to pass*
a test   it's not for everyone

if you eat a mouthful of dirt you can go
I eat the dirt –
the boys run off with the tyre

an ordinary day

a Sunday visit to the Arnolds' farm
Gwen takes Mum straight to the kitchen
men and kids inspect sheep and cows

times are better – the farm now
has a live-in couple with a young child
help for both Harry and Gwen

silent and heavy   the farmhand follows
Dad and Harry into the kitchen for tea
sits apart   listening as they wait

his little boy totters across the room
to climb the mountain of his father's legs
tries again and again   ignored by the big man

the toddler finally reaches his goal
        balances briefly
                then falls

        the man doesn't move

Murray

it's New Year's Eve
    all the shops are open
Dad talks to farmers in his office
Brian and I join the other kids
    racing through the dark lane
and the vacant block by the Bank
I stop any adult I pass to announce
    I've got a new brother

when Dad takes us to the hospital
    our Mum is so tired
we don't stay long
we don't meet Murray Leigh

the worst of having a baby in the house
    is SAGO   the favoured infant food
thickly coated inside a large enamel mug
it waits each night for my dishwashing chore

the best is pushing Murray in his pram
    around the streets after school
arriving at the rise beside Streaders
    letting the pram run down the slope
and catching it before it crashes
    into the State Rivers fence

sheep

she's only nine but she can work the dogs!
Dad boasts to his mates

sun wind and singing birds for companions
I walk with him along country roads
                    behind the mob
when he goes back for the car I'm in charge
but really   I can't control the dogs

today I'm trusted to move the sheep
to a paddock
        on the far side of the channel
the sheep baulk at the narrow bridge
            scatter along the bank
I shout at the dog
        he leaps at the sheep
                the sheep scatter more
I run one way   dog the other
        herding them back past the bridge
                    again and again
hot exhausted crying   I'm alone in the universe

a miracle: one sheep ventures onto the bridge
another follows
            cautiously a few more
I hold my breath
        the rest saunter across into the paddock
the dog smug as if it's his success

I rush to shut the gate
            throw myself under a tree

Dad keeps boasting of his daughter

the bad grandfather

I never saw my grandfather drunk
nor heard him yelling in the street
never saw my grandmother
hiding the knives   bruises on her face

on Sunday evenings he came to tea
stayed with us for the Lux Radio Play
until Dad drove him home
to his little room behind the pub

he taught me how to count sheep
hand slicing the air to separate a group
for each hundred he moved a matchstick
from left hand to right

birdsong and a smiling blue sky
little girl admiring and content
capable grandfather in charge
sheep leaping at the gate

. . . First and Third Thursdays

Australian born

youngest of his family
    dressed in velvet and lace
my bad grandfather
    Albert Edward
is named for Queen Victoria's playboy son

though our ancestors in the Fens
    took 200 years to migrate six miles
Bertie's parents sail
    12,000 miles in five months of 1852
to settle into busy lives in Geelong

his father is Town Surveyor and an architect
his mother runs a small school
    in their comfortable large house
with its conservatory and croquet lawn

Methodism is the fabric of their lives
the home filled
    with tea meetings and hymns
the boys' upbringing is strict:
    cold baths and temperance meetings
softened for Bertie by his mother's favour

he is fifteen when his mother dies
    her desertion casting long shadows
he starts drinking at eighteen
a jaunty young chap with a fine baritone voice
    who prefers parties to church

'the belle of Geelong'

my grandmother Millie's parents
travel on the same ship as
          Bertie's parents
though they never meet
          through five long months at sea

Millie's mother Ann   *base born*
          (as the birth record proclaims)
comes from the *closed* village of Helmingham
          where the lord owns all the land
provides good housing and plots for workers
who keep 'high moral standards':
          single pregnant girls must leave
          if not   the whole family is expelled

Ann at nineteen gives birth in a nearby village
five years later she marries a handsome labourer
          after seven years they move
with their four children to Australia:
          three months work at Burumbeet
          for 40 pounds and rations
          before freedom to settle in Geelong

          quiet respectable and private
they live two streets away from Bertie's family
          attend the same church   do not intrude
their fifth daughter Millicent Louisa is born in 1859
the same year as her brother
drowns in the Barwon

Millie grows up to be responsible and loving
          stays home to help her widowed mother
yet is visible enough to be called
          'the belle of Geelong'

Promises

to their families' surprise
      Bertie courts the saintly Millie
takes her for drives in a hired carriage
      presents her with a book
The Language and Poetry of Flowers

charmed by her debonair suitor
she tells a friend
      he has style
      and a great pair of hands
      with the horses

they marry in their shared Wesleyan church
      Bertie is twenty-two
      Millie eleven years older
      though admitting to nine

they rent a fine 'gentleman's residence'
Millie is *At Home   First and Third Thursdays*
      Bertie works as a contractor
      stars in comedy songs and sketches

two years later
      they sell all their furniture and stock
Millie moves to her father-in-law's big house
      Bertie goes 200 miles north for work

the red scarf

you come from the north in a shining gig
        wearing a smart Chesterfield coat
a red scarf at your throat like a banner

Doris your three-year-old daughter
            runs to meet you
remembers the feeling 90 years later

Millie thrills to your cocky charm   the life
        it brings to your father's house
you break the rhythm of her busy days
        as mother to your daughters
housekeeper to your sociable father
        nurse to your bedridden sister

they delight when you work in the garden
but perseverance was
            never your strength
they expect little
            are not disappointed
you love Millie   she loves you
waits for your next unsettling appearance

Boort 1898

when Bertie's father dies
    the big house is sold
the invalid sent to a married sister
Millie is free to join Bertie in Boort
    after four years of being apart

no pioneer outpost:
climbing over the end of Bald Hill
    Boort is now a three-pub town
boasting besides blacksmiths and stores
    two resident doctors
    three visiting dentists
    two solicitors
    three music teachers
    and a piano tuner

Bertie and Millie and their two daughters live
in Uncle John's substantial house
    next to his large flour mill
when John *gets too familiar*
    Millie flees to her sister nearby
Bertie is again a casual visitor
until he rents a place near the railway
with four rooms   hessian ceilings

(in the big drought of 1902
    so much dust collected
in the neighbours' ceiling that it broke
almost suffocating the sleeping couple below)

two sons are born to the new residents
    the family is now complete
Bertie delighted with his hectic social life
Millie content in her quiet home retreat

the tablespoons

I'm looking for Millie in *The Boort Standard*:
six hundred weekly editions
since she and Bertie settled here

Bertie is easy to find among Federation debates
the Boer War   bushfires   drownings
rainfall and the state of crops and roads –

he appears in the sporting columns   the reports
of concerts and civic events
the Glee Club   the Minstrel Troupe
Hospital Sunday   donor of citizenship prizes
his business advertised on the front page

just two brief entries for Millie   years apart
helping at a rowing regatta in one
finally   last in a list of wedding guests
I read her name   her gift:
                          tablespoons

the onlooker

an eight-year-old girl meets Millie and Bertie in 1906–1909
speaks of it 90 years later

Doris's father was very highly thought of but he was an alcoholic. He was a very clever man and a good civic-minded man too. He was a gentleman. There's a difference. You can have a man who's drunk in the street and he's a hobo and no good but Mr B was a gentleman.

Millie wasn't a big woman. They were very nice people. They probably didn't mix much – perhaps it was no money. There was a definite social scale even among the tradespeople. Someone asked my aunt what the new bank teller was like. She said she didn't know – she hadn't seen him eat.

Sometimes Grandma would say to me, I think we'll go and see dear Millie today. It would look as if we were going with a basket of flowers but underneath it would be groceries and things, might be a pound of butter and there were always toys. She'd have a black eye and look awful but it wasn't darling Bertie, it was the demon drink.

I thought demons and devils had horns and I couldn't apply that to darling Bertie. I'd go down the street and when I met him he'd always give me a hug and I couldn't see any horns or pitchforks. The men were into all kinds of sports and they covered up for him.

Sweet Millie would have nothing to do with the races, gambling and that sort of thing. Millie had beautiful furniture, early Victorian you know. Carving in the settee. Lovely walnut suite. She sold it very cheaply.

home truths

from Doris's diary 1909–1911

1 Jan 1909   *I've not written anything about Father (at a time like this I feel as if I can't say Dad). This is the third week he has been drinking and nearly every day he has come home drunk. Dad threatens to kill himself every day and today he hit mother. We are so glad he does not go shooting.*

12 Jun 1909   *I always thought but now I know that I have for my father a brute and a coward. At first it was that bitter that I couldn't speak.*

16 Nov 1909   *Life is awfully sad - I find Dad has been drinking for about 3 or 6 weeks now. I'm getting more frightened at night, when he comes home, that I can't sleep. Today he told mother he'd kill her.*

14 Mar 1910   *Father has been awful lately - for about 5 weeks. Drunk at dinnertime and again at teatime in fact - never sober. The effects are not off him when he rises. Our outlook seems more drear than ever. Always this never ending struggle for necessaries.*

27 Mar 1910   *Fan gave me a Teddy Bear hat pin last week. I do wish the hotelkeepers would keep their gifts for all the time I feel they are paid for with the money which we ought to have.*

30 Jul 1910   *Prospects are awfully dull at present. Dad hasn't a thing on hand and every penny, perhaps the last, that comes in goes to the hotel. He's awfully down and at times melancholy.*

15 Apr 1911   *A man that through his own folly keeps you and his family in the depths of poverty, makes his wife's hair turn grey with worry, tells you to clear out, wrings your hands until you scream, turns his drunken fingers round your throat like a murderer, and vows he'll kill the whole family* *and chases his daughter round the room shouting, 'I'll kill her'. No wonder the word 'father' makes one shudder. That drink! What won't it do? Ruins homes, wrecks men's lives, breaks wives' hearts, and turns children into wrecks of men and women*

Millie

when Bertie lost control of the demon drink
I kept telling the angry children
         he has only one fault

as work and money dried up
         I kept my standards
house tidy and spotless in spite of dust
children too:
         dresses done up   shoes clean
         never open the door in an apron dear
         a lady never leaves home without gloves
         don't hold bitterness   speak gently
the children made me proud
as they left to begin their life's work

when cancer invaded my breast
Bertie took me to Melbourne for treatment
         I know now I will never return
my children care for me wonderfully
         in a flat they rent
I am so lucky with family and friends
but how I miss Bertie   his occasional visits
         the highlight of my days

the red scarf ii

By small margins, perhaps, we find our way
or lose it.   Diane Fahey

once Millie left for Melbourne
the landlord sold the house over your head
        I'd never sell while
        Mrs B needed a roof
you rented a room at McNeill's Coffee Palace
        sat with cronies smoking on benches outside

when the Palace closed
        Bill gave you a job in his business
preparing accounts in perfect copperplate
helping with the sheep he bought
        you lived in rooms behind the office
        burnt it down with your pipe

you moved to a small room behind the pub
        once used to display salesmen's samples
sitting with mates under the peppertree nearby
you waved your walking stick as I passed

when war came and we left Boort
the family arranged for Care in Melbourne
        your final home before hospital
was an iron bed and small cabinet
                in a bare dormitory

as cancer gripped your throat
your voice a whisper
you wanted no alcohol
only cold rain on your tongue

on our last visit   you stood by the bed
leaning on your stick
slowly lifted your hand in farewell
a red scarf round your throat like a wound

. . . the earthiness of heaven

seismic

sent for by the Headmaster
    during Geography class
I hurried out:
    your baby brother is in hospital
    you and Brian will stay
    at my house after school
    until your parents come

with hardly a thought for the sick boy
I swaggered back to my seat
    feeling special
kids never went to the Head's place

we read books till Dad came to take us
    to our neighbours the Marshalls
with no word of the hospital drama unfolding:
    equipment the little boy needed
had been lent to Quambatook
    a makeshift contraption must be used

Mrs Marshall cooked a special cake for tea
    tried hard to make things normal
we slept in the distant front room
under the stern sepia gaze of dead Mr Marshall

Dad woke us early   his face crumpled
his mouth tight:
    Murray's dead
and then
    my strong father cried

sea air

Catherine wheels   rockets   Roman candles
our cousin Jock lights these on Guy Fawkes Night
   in the courtyard of Uncle Hal's empire –
paradise to kids who usually explode
a few firecrackers in the backyard
   please to remember
   the fifth of November
   gunpowder treason and plot

we're here after our baby brother's so sudden death
   the sea air and change of scene
   will do wonders for your mother's health
the pervasive air of the holiday is not kelp
and beneficial *ozone*   but bread

bakers with long-handled shovels
place dough and retrieve bread from the huge ovens
at the back of the courtyard
   the open fire box   scene from a friendly hell
   backdrop to devouring fresh hot bread
magic to live above a shop selling such treats
     and to visit another on Main Street
where cakes pastries and soft drinks are given as we ask

one day we smear thousands of eggs
                with greasy KeepEgg
roll them sensuously in our hands
        place them in large tins for the future
Dad and Hal sit chatting and smearing
easy together though now they seldom meet

we leave as carts are being filled
                for outlying townships
smell the sweat of horses and fresh dung –
        the earthiness of heaven

on Monday mornings

two columns of smoke rise from Boort houses
    breakfasts are cooked on one fire
laundry coppers boil above the other

steaming sheets heaved from copper to tub
through wringer to rinsing tub
      brilliant with Reckitt's Blue
wringer again   extra dip into starch for some
    heavy baskets carried to the yard
washing lifted onto the line
    for fresh fabrics to dance in the wind

    one Friday Mum's friend Peg
decides she needs cash
    more than the tax man
brings home the shop takings before golf
    stuffs notes into the laundry firebox
against non-existent robbers
    rushes to the first hole

her helper Nellie Beattie arrives on Monday
lights the copper fire
    and the smoke rises
richer and darker into the laughing blue sky

'he's my brother'

a commotion in the schoolyard
    as I set off home for lunch
a kid screaming   others gathered around
a shout – my name   my young brother
    is doubled in pain on the ground

I race to him
    lift him on my back
start in a stumbling run along the hill
my panic rising
    when a magpie swoops
I weave   and almost fall

Brian's constant crying drives me on
bent under his weight
    I plunge downhill
and along the road until I reach the kitchen
hand all the terror to my mother –
    and a twisted bowel rights itself

years later
    I wonder why I didn't carry him
the few metres to the teachers' room
realise I never thought of anywhere
    but home

'He Ain't Heavy, He's My Brother', The Hollies 1969

is it raining on Lyndger?

when rain fell on our iron roof
my father would go to the door to look
towards his distant paddock by the lake:
is it raining on Lyndger?

since the first settlers began farming
weather has ruled our lives
too much   too little   too heavy   too light
wrong place   wrong time
is it raining on Lyndger?

the winner of the newspaper's
Most Unlikely Headline once read:
Farmers Satisfied
I accept the slander   true but unjust
is it raining on Lyndger?

later in the city I hardly knew whether
the moon had a halo to bring the rain
was it upright at the quarter to tip it out
or a crescent to hold it in?

choosing coat or umbrella my main concern
never thought of the rain on Lake Lyndger

kindling

sun's up in our quiet town   I'm lying
on my parents' bed listening
to their casual talk as they dress

argument begins over the kitchen fire:
Mum will light it if there's kindling
which Dad hasn't chopped

today they move to a new topic:
who will be first to die
meaning   who has worked hardest

I realise that one of them will be right

many years later in the little Hills cemetery
my children's father shows me
his chosen plot with the expansive view

we stand together companionably
we rarely argued in the past   don't now
I recall that earlier scene and realise
                    that one of us . . .

marbles

Dad's friend teased me that Jimmy Baker
was my boyfriend   I hated it –
Jimmy   a dirty boy with patched clothes

Jimmy's dad was a shearer   a starvation job
with sheep sold for a shilling a head
but I had no sympathy

I worried for Lorna   a skinny kid unkempt hair
crumpled clothes   whose crippled mother
sewed for a living in a shopfront flat

when marbles season inevitably came round
Jimmy shone   though it didn't soften my heart
I thrived too   my bag always full

Lorna's tiny pouch was so near empty
that one day I offered to play for her
took her few tors to the ring   and lost the lot

Sunday School

after the midday roast   a long walk
      to the little wooden church
its pitched roof distant kin
      to the cathedrals of Europe

the cane birthday chair in the vestry
      is laced with ribbons for Kinder Class
camels donkeys and white robed people
      move on a sand tray towards Bethlehem
or become felt shapes on the new flannelgraph
each week we leave singing
      goodbye goodbye we will be kind and true

we graduate to pews in the church
      girls to left   boys to right
rewarded for knowledge of Bible texts
      with garish stamps
which never make it to my treasures tin

I learn boredom listening to repeated Bible stories
Zaccheus my favourite – small   curious
      finally winning attention!
at the anniversary   we wear new clothes
sit on flimsy tiers behind the pulpit
      feeding my fear of falling

    on my last day of Sunday School
Mrs Thomas gives me a small New Testament
like those carried in soldiers' pockets
      to deflect bullets
on the flyleaf she has written
      For Miriel, to me a real pal
I'm surprised   pleased   very guilty

pomegranate

beside a pomegranate tree in the churchyard
Bess   the Sunday School Superintendent's daughter
        and the minister's daughter Joy
argue over whose father owns the church
    I'm silent
    my father doesn't even go to church

outside Nafplio in Greece
        a pomegranate tree
guards Hera's sacred spring
men come in carloads to bottle the water
      for their wives to drink:
the goddess promises fertility

no one told us the pomegranate
        was Hera's symbol
or that there *were* goddess-worshipping days
    before a Father and Son supplanted them
we early learnt that mothers don't own churches

table talk

Brian and I sit
  at the long side of the table
    parents at each end
we talk of school and work
the parents begin to argue
     angry words fly
Mum hurls a loaf of bread
     Dad evades
  we're thunderstruck

I'm older for the next fight
     perhaps ten
Mum says she's leaving
    and storms from the table
slams the front door my stomach knots
Dad settles beside the fire
     with the paper
I'm furious that he's not chasing her
I'm scared –
   why isn't he chasing her?
at bed time
  we find her lying on their bed
Dad knew she had nowhere to go

the white cliffs

plates heavy with cold lamb and pickles
lamingtons   sponge rolls   jelly cakes
    Sunday tea at district farms –
Robertsons Suttons Loaders Slatters

the hosts came out at the sound
          of motor and dogs
mothers went inside to prepare
    and chat of children   ailments   CWA
men and kids walked to the paddock
where Pud drove trotters around a track
or off to the yards where sheep waited
        for crutching or Shows

mice plagues made barns and stacks boil
    droughts threatened animals and roses
dust storms swept so much topsoil away
    a roadside sign appeared:
        caution farm crossing

after the meal
    men talked horses and crops at the fire
women washed dishes in a bowl on the table
before moving to the piano for songs of empire:
    the white cliffs of Dover
    pack up your troubles
    wish me luck as you wave me goodbye

when the candles burnt low in their sconces
we left our friends and drove under bright stars
through mallee or wildly gesticulating lignum
    the moon always rising

two Majors

my grandmother Sarah   the Salvation Army Major
    came from Sydney when I was ten
she sat up in bed   round jolly and going bald
    laughing often   her eyes crinkled
she taught me only one song: *Fire a Volley Amen*

hard to picture her as the 24-year-old Captain
    sent in 1894 with another young woman
to open the Army cause in a gold-mining town –
      10,000 souls to be saved
her motto:
    when the outlook is grim
    try the uplook
The Lord never let her down
    since whatever He did was perfect

her daughter Major Sadie visited from Perth
    gentle and obedient as a little girl
(never an accomplice
    in my mother's childhood crimes)
a kind and loving adult   an accomplished nurse

she had sent us western wildflowers
    now brought me a serviette ring
with a picture of the Sydney Harbour Bridge
What lovely hands she said
    when I massaged her aching head

she was matron of a Home where single
        mothers came to hide and give birth
working hard to pay for their keep
she watched over these young women
        saw them parted from their babies
died at forty-seven of overwork   and sadness

the national religion

1938's winter was enlivened by Bradman
and Ashes Tests in England
    as the world lurched towards war
newspaper headlines were devoted to cricket
Jenny Holmes made a scrapbook for me
        with cuttings of each team
my precious Bible for years

we kids were in bed before the broadcasts began
    kept listening through two shut doors
ABC radio was serious – when the cables came in
commentators reported each ball
        each stroke as if they were there
pencil on wood made a perfect bat on ball

Dad often turned to 3DB   they had no pretensions
    provided jokes and songs between cables
when the song Rickety Kate announced a wicket
    I rushed to the closed door to hear more details
returned shivering to tell my six-year-old brother
    only to find him asleep

I remained awake   loyal to Bradman and the boys
now blame cricket and the demons in the quince tree
    for my lifelong insomnia

sportsgirl

I never lost my title Best in Street
at cricket and football
I relinquished it

how did I know?
no one told me at twelve it was now
impossible to play with the boys

fortunately tennis remained   we played
before school   after school   early on Saturday
later   in the adults' district competition

Saturday mornings also included hand-beating
sponge cakes   our share of the afternoon teas
carried in suitcases held flat by the women

our family played for Boort Ramblers
drove to Yando   Leagher or Catumnal
Barrapoort or Terrapee

my parents played mixed doubles together
argued every point at home
then it was my turn

Dad recounted every mistake
at 40-30 you should've gone down the line
I accepted the tuition   loved the attention

school holiday

for Lesley

your house was small   sheltered
by willows along the channel
mud around the milking shed
salt rising in the paddocks

that first evening of my visit
we sat around the fire reading
until you said *let's go to the creek*
I was amazed – it was almost bedtime
more amazed when your mother agreed

silent paddocks   dreamy moonlight
the creek a wide lake of lustrous grey
                in a very wide world
an old rowboat carried us
between ghostly trunks of drowned river gums
the only sound the plip and gurgle of oars
            and the occasional stirring of a bird –
my first night out on water
                under a full moon

after midnight we returned to the house
to your mother still reading Dickens by the fire
            made cocoa and toast before bed
another midnight first

did I sleep that night
or was the universe too wide?

Sunny South

my father pruned the Alistair Clark rose
        covering half the veranda
the bushy shape and large open flowers
unlike the standard roses along the path

on Sundays in early summer
after a week lumping bags of grain
        he walked around his roses
like God in the Garden of Eden

on autumn Sundays I followed
        as he and his friend Harry
studied each bloom   each scent
pondered every blemish

when years later I visit the town
        the Sunny South has gone
but Dad and his friend still walk
with me in rose gardens

Sept 3rd 1939

Sunday evenings Mum goes to church
Dad stays home to talk with his father
but strangely today   Dad too goes to church

listening to the new Lux Radio Theatre
Brian and I sit with Grandpa on the couch
still in its winter position In front of the fire

suddenly the producer interrupts the drama
 to announce *We are at war with Germany*
and the play goes on

when our parents return
we remember our news   lift our eyes
we're at war and return to the play

at once Dad strides to the radio
switches to ABC and hears Mr Menzies
repeat his message again and again

no one speaks
the old man and the young miffed
not to hear the end of the play

Eng Lit

intense heat always began with the new school year
      come February our legs stuck to seats
our arms to desks as our heads lay on our hands

we survived the mornings of maths and science
faltered in the drowsy periods after lunch –
         History Geography English:
Nobly, nobly Cape St Vincent to the north-west died away;
Sunset ran, one glorious blood red, streaking into Cadiz Bay;

each evening sunset ran blood-red over Hospital Hill
blazing behind the steep roof
               of the Catholic church
but it wasn't the same – to our north-west lay
only Quambatook Terrapee Barrapoort

in Room 2 Mr Rogan sat at the table facing us
he put his hand to his sweating forehead
      'Turn to page 31:
      The Burial of Sir John Moore at Corunna
      Hercules you begin'

Hercules no hero struggled from his desk:
      Not a drum was heard not a funeral note
      As his corpse to the rampart we hurried
he managed the first verse in our ritual singsong
then:
      We buried him darkly at dead of night
      The sods of our bayonets turning

'No Hercules   the sods <u>with</u> our bayonets turning'
we never turned sods   we dug or we ploughed
'Try again.'
>   *We buried him darkly at dead of night*
>   *The sods of our bayonets turning*

Mr Rogan looked up   suspicious
was this deliberate? 'Once more.'
>   *We buried him darkly at dead of night*
>   *The sods of our bayonets turning*

Mr Rogan gave up
'Lanyon continue'
Lanyon mumbled the next verse:
>   *No useless coffin enclosed his breast,*
>   *Nor in sheet nor in shroud we wound him;*
>   *But he lay like a warrior taking his rest,*
>   *His material cloak around him.*

Mr Rogan sighed   he spoke very softly
>   through clenched teeth
'martial cloak, Lanyon, martial.'
on this day I believe   he decided to join the Air Force

metaphors

for Susan Hampton

yes, the Book of Revelation holds
rich and powerful metaphors
just not for me

at ten   I cowered in my sleep-out bed
peeking in terror from under the sheets
lest Jesus appear in clouds over Bald Hill

with metal feet   eyes of fire
from his mouth   a sharp two-edged sword
in his hand the keys of death and hell

the war began   the Middle East a battle zone
the place for Armageddon
our minister was sure the end was near

expert on God and War – an ambulance
orderly in the first great war –
he knew that 666 meant Hitler

war ended   Jesus and Armageddon didn't come
I left the sleep-out and our country town
sometime later left the metaphors

after Dunkirk

my father stands in the middle of the kitchen
the warmest room in the cold house
     his brother's letter in his hand
silently he passes it to my mother
I read over her shoulder:

> *Dear Bill*
> *It seems things are getting serious*
> *I wonder what you're thinking*
> *I feel I must go so in the years ahead*
> *Jock won't have to*
> *If we enlist together in Melbourne*
> *we could stay together . . .*
> *Love, Hal*

our quiet kitchen becomes quieter:
the pause before a storm breaks
     my chest is tight

within a month they are in the army
and our lives change forever

power again

the day Dad went to war
Mum let the chooks out
just opened the gate
and said *shoo*

that afternoon Mrs Marshall came over
to say our hens had joined hers
    she'd bring them back later

Mrs Marshall please keep them
I'd love you to have them

she'd always hated squawking chooks
feeding   watering   gathering eggs
at Show time Dad washing them
in Reckitt's Blue in her spotless laundry
        never again

she moved house   sold a house   bought a house
returned to her passion for teaching

war

woodheap blocks became our backyard fort
    an old car the perfect tank
we crawled on our bellies over desert sands
marched   saluted   presented arms

Boort was a conservative and patriotic town
willing to fight for God and King:
the Home Guard practised forming an avenue
    of headlights so lost or wounded planes
        could land on our main road
we accepted the ancient Roman saying
    if you wish for peace, prepare for war

    in high school I read an essay
challenging those words:
if you wish for peace, prepare for peace
I was persuaded   no longer would Dad
    and Boort be my political guides

my final break with received wisdom came
    when I read Rudyard Kipling
that great champion of military virtues:
after his son died in the First World War
he spoke for all the dead soldiers:
If any question why we died
Tell them because our fathers lied

'in the years ahead'
my brother and cousin did not go to war
they grew up fatherless at important times
how can we measure the cost
    of Dad's absence   Hal's death?

my brother's war effort

i *The Boort Standard* *3 Sep 1940*
Tobacco Tin Derby

Saturday's Tobacco Tin Derby culminated with a grand total of 6443 tins being made available to the Red Cross . . . a fine achievement by the boys. . . . Vic Thorpe of the Commercial Hotel sponsored the Derby and gave prizes and refreshments to contestants which will raise nearly £3 for the Red Cross.

The winner collected 1460 tins. Brian, thanks to the selfless contributions of his father and grandfather, came an honourable sixth out of fifteen with 340 tins.

ii *plane spotting*

After our move to Bendigo in 1941, Brian joined the Volunteer Air Observers' Corps with a classmate:

We had to pass a test to identify all sorts of aircraft, theirs and ours, in case our pilots got lost, or the Japanese flew over the continent without detection.

Test passed, we were allowed to take our place on the observation tower, a mine poppet head on top of a hill in Rosalind Park. Our watch was 2–4 pm on Friday. A hut was built on the second landing, which kept out a fraction of the icy wind. The radiator was out of action – the element fused when used as a pie warmer. We also had a telephone connected to Headquarters, and a couple of chairs with the stuffing gone.

We had an adrenalin rush every shift when the mail plane to Kerang flew overhead. Frantically we phoned HQ to assure them it was safe for the plane to continue.

In spite of the fact that we never reported any enemy aircraft, when the conflict ended we were each awarded a medal and a certificate.

leaving

1941: Dad the soldier is in training
Mum applies to teach again
insisting on a high school town
so we could finish school from home

what presentiment led my father
to lease his farm for ten years
my mother to sell the house
before our move to Bendigo?

Winter: a cold and wet July
packing crates on the back veranda
mud and wood shavings mingled
Dad arrives on Final Leave

we travel together to Bendigo
that first night in a hotel
a special treat for Brian and me
unaware of our parents' mood

next day Mum laughs her thanks
to Nellie Melba who   years before
stopped the town clock's chimes
at midnight . . . no emotion today

on his way to service overseas
the soldier catches his train
we look for a house to rent
and Boort becomes a place

. . . sounds below the birdsong

reading the papers

I was the first of my family to return
spending term holidays
    on a farm just north of Boort
where my Infant Room goddess
had married Dad's best man

the goddess became Freda my friend
    we gathered eggs
under sheds and farm machinery
inspected dusty cedar furniture
    bought at district clearing sales
now on hooks along barn walls
    awaiting restoration

occasionally we played tennis
    or sat in the den where newspapers
piled up for weeks beside Freda's chair
    to be read in order   earliest on top

at my wedding I wore
    her exquisite lace dress
        her veil hiding my face
used her gift of silverware
through twenty-two years of marriage

when my mother died in another State
Freda raced her Mercedes to be there

the plantation

when holidaying with Freda and Jack
I fell in love with wide paddocks gentle rises
      mallee everywhere
I rode in the jinker with Jack   checking the sheep
     their toddler John playing at our feet

as we passed the plantation that marked his birth
I pictured the boy one day farming these paddocks
     his grandfather was the first ever to plough
perhaps John's children too would farm here –
four generations
      unlike Dad's nomadic family

it was years before I learnt of the Dja Dja Wurrung
whose stories were the history of these lands
     here for two thousand generations

the brothers

enlisting as old men aged 38 and 40
after the age limits were raised
Bill and Hal relished their fitness
their mates   their training
they refused promotion to avoid separation
        in this 'happiest time of our lives'

separation came in Malaya's jungles
as the Japanese swiftly advanced south
Bill was invalided home missing an eye
        Hal imprisoned in Changi

we're excited to welcome Dad in Melbourne
after his wild voyage on a tramp steamer
strange to meet a sick man
        guilty at leaving his friends before battle
anxious to rejoin the army and train soldiers
        who might rescue his brother

thin and wiry   Hal survived Changi
        and the move to Borneo
too ill to be sent on the Death Marches
        he was left to die in Sandakan
a survivor told of a friendship that grew
        between Hal and a younger man
as together they faced sickness and death

Hal died four months before war ended
        the Sabah people say his spirit rests
with their warriors
        on Kinabalu   the sacred mountain

back to Boort

my parents took ten years to return
waiting after war ended
for that long lease to expire

twenty years after Eve's vow and Bill's promise
never to ask her to live on a farm
they moved to his Leaghur property

once again she left the teaching she loved
and in her fifties fed horses dogs chooks and shearers
at least never learnt to milk the cow

she carried water in buckets to begin a garden
(irrigating flowers being low on Bill's list)
eventually the water flowed
the garden a sanctuary

forty years after her death
I return to the empty house now falling back to earth
the garden derelict   a few bushes struggling

but the claret ash   centrepiece of Eve's creation
still broadcasts its rich autumn colour
to the sombre grey-green of the home paddock

red blossoms

I see you walking your hard-won land
from native pines and mallee sands
in the cleared paddocks
            to red gums on the river
and the crab-holed black box plains
                around the lake

do you hear sounds below the birdsong
as you take visitors to see
                the canoe tree's scar?
you dig middens for your roads
        great stuff for boggy country

can you see ghosts behind
                the green-grey canopies?
those initiated by losing a tooth
        who called this place *Le-aar ghur*:
red blossoms or the bleeding tooth

                in the new century
I buy red poppies for you on Remembrance Day

golden years

when the hard work was done
and you retired to town
you struggled with emphysema
driving the few yards to the shops

you rang farmers with machines
organised their working bees
for a swimming pool in town
a new plantation for the road

Legacy and Returned Soldiers took
your energy – your duty to those
who didn't return
        or came back maimed

though you never once complained
        of pain and limitation
your biting words could hurt our mother
you knew how to twist the knife –
        she always fell

whenever she planned to visit her sisters
        at the last moment   you were ill
my brother asked her why she stayed
        she was so surprised
oh Brian we've had such wonderful times

hierarchy

just before his 70th birthday
my father wrote to me in Fiji
I would place as highlights in my life
1   marriage to old Caro
(family name for our mother)
2   the birth of you three nips
3   our visit to you Fijians
the last quite a recent event

pity I didn't show this to Caro
who believed Dad's hierarchy to be
dog first
horse second
she hoped she was third

visitor

odd to be looking for my parents' new house
　　since they left the farm for town

the house is big – plenty of room for grandchildren
the formal rooms filled with solid Victorian furniture
French polished by Dad　a skill learnt in Army rehab

the town is changing
my classmates have vanished
the people I see are my mother's friends
I no longer know the shopkeepers

we return every three years for a short stay
as my children grow　so too their memories:
picking apricots from the garage roof
gorging on them from big baskets in the sun room
feet burning on asphalt streets to the swimming pool
buying jubes to help Grandpop stop smoking
watching TV not seen in Fiji　learning the jingles
hearing a church service in English

the schoolyard

1910   my father the schoolboy
plants a sugar gum tree
one of a row along the top fence

1925   my mother the teacher
plants a sugar gum in a plantation
on the flank of Bald Hill

1939   my father's gum is a giant
my mother's is one of the striplings
on the side of Hospital Hill

on Arbor Day I plant a sugar gum
beside the headmaster's house
near the hospital

1963   on one of our family visits
my daughter starts school
in the same classroom as Dad and I

his eucalypt has gone
Mum's is there but hardly grows
a struggling gum *may* be mine

Arbor Day no longer happens
my daughter doesn't plant a tree

foreshore

always the same   always different:
a new swimming pool
            beside the Little Lake
plaques of Australia's Prime Ministers
line the path
            from pool to tennis courts
and spindly native trees
            replace the willows
shading us between matches

the once tranquil Little Lake is filled
with skiers behind noisy boats
            scores of cabins line the waterfront
in Nolan's Park a massive stone
            shaped like the Matterhorn
has come from Switzerland
            to honour early pioneers

high school students have made a path
            around half the Big Lake
I follow it to a wide treeless space
            near Kinypanial Creek
at my feet a collection
            of quartz chippings
where the Yung Balug clan once made tools

do kids still catch yabbies in the channel?

the Railway Hotel

a hundred years later I'm visiting
    my grandfather's drinking hole
    some things haven't changed
    the bar on Saturday night still blokey
    portraits of boozy men on the walls
    their grandsons at the bar
    hell bent on becoming them

today I'm to lunch at the widows' table:
a group of cheerful women meet at noon
for a $5 roast dinner
        extra dollar for coffee
they talk of charities families gardens
        then return to empty houses
        and eggs for tea

free of alcohol
I fall down the front steps of the pub

. . . the grey-green horizon

revelation

I fashioned a tragic figure of you
not from your hilarious tales
but with bones from your sister's stories
flesh from my own flawed view

a toddler hiding from your drunken father
bright scholar leaving school at thirteen
alone in town with that pitiable father
your beloved mother's long illness
the hard Depression years

cost of war to you old soldier
an eye and a brother left in the jungle
the guilt of leaving your men behind
a ten-year struggle to breathe
huge nightmare fireballs coming again

when cancer came you seemed resigned
an extra thirty years you said
thinking of your brother Hal
Smithy   Frank   and half the regiment

in drama class one night I acted you
hitched up my pants
pushed the hat back on my head
whistled the border collie to my side
and sauntered behind the sheep

lost in each flowering bush and tree
each nesting zebra finch
the colours of a rainbow bird

meeting

twenty years
after his death
he comes towards me
on the path

grey hair
military walk
same tentative
carriage of the head

for a millisecond
I start to run to him
wish I had
when I could

witch

when the time has come for a child to sever its ties
with the mother . . . the mother will appear a witch.

Erich Neumann

are you a witch   mother my love
your wrinkled hands restless in the tidy room?
the broomstick's been there all my life
not used for flying but repelling dirt
our neat world braced against the earth

you did your duty without complaint
your house and children *perfect*
still try to tell me what to wear and eat
had less control of Bill it seemed

and yet you keep a laughing innocence
at 74 you said *I still feel twelve*
        you have a simple wisdom
        help whoever comes
        want to accept the new

never were our ties severed   Caro my love
just comfort-loosened   made of silk

adieu

tired from the long flight
terrified of what I might see
I crept up the stairs after my brother

the nun smiled as she eased
your body into its tranquil pose
your arm curled on the pillow
like the girl you always were
the wedding ring still tight
on your twisted finger
bury it with her   we decide

you stay asleep
safe in your Father's kingdom

no alabaster

below the crematorium chimney
guarded by tea-tree and callistemon
my mother is buried
in a patchwork of lawn and flowers

between Father Gilbert and Mr Coat
with ex-AIF Anderson at her head
the regulation plaque has few words:
her name   two dates   *Gone Home*

she belonged to no place
lived by her father's text
here we have no continuing city
she expected that other

death is natural she said
consoling us when our father died
so when death came for her
alone at home   naturally   in the night

I must believe she went in trust
would be content that ducks
ibis and plovers feed on the grass
above her bones

dulce domum

driving south on the Murray Valley highway
Ruth and I are following the river
        from mouth to source
we're great on holidays – could this be our 500th?

past Swan Hill and the lakes
        past Kerang and the Loddon
flat paddocks   mallee slopes   varied crops
        no tourist spectaculars here
we chat   are silent   start singing
        the hymns and carols of years past
finally   triumphantly   Handel's Messiah

I'm half asleep in the afternoon sun
        the miles roll on
suddenly I'm shocked
        with a sense of something familiar
and break the silence:
        this reminds me of home
my birthplace a mere twenty k's away

I'm puzzled
        is it the grey-green horizon
those untidy semi-circles of black box
        the wide sky that calls me?

unlike Mole in *The Wind in the Willows*
        we don't turn aside   we keep to our plan
but it's there

Acknowledgements

My sincere thanks to those, led by my brother, who have jogged my failing memory of earlier times. Jennifer Weaver and Helen Storey of the Boort Historical Society have been most helpful with all my queries. My brother allowed me to use his recollections of wartime experiences, and my cousin, Helen, gave permission for the use of her mother's diaries.

I am grateful for the perceptive comments and generous support of my writing colleagues Louise Crisp, Diane Fahey, Jill Golden, Annette Marner, Margaret Merrilees, Julia Parkin, Robin Parkin and Ruth Raintree.

Wakefield Press has made this, my seventh book with them, as pleasurable an experience as the others. Thank you Michael Bollen, Margot Lloyd, Clinton Ellicott, Liz Nicholson and the rest of the team.

sun wind & diesel
Miriel Lenore

Where, or rather how, does anyone belong?

In this book, Miriel Lenore reflects on her life in two places –
a Ngaanyatjarra community in the desert where she is a
visitor, and her home in Adelaide with family and friends. To
these people and places, she brings a sharp eye, her political
and historical lenses and wry humour to create deceptively
simple poems with many layered meanings. In her poems,
the land always carries its complex and particular history, as
she interweaves her responses to the natural world with the
deliberate relationships between people and the continuing
effects of the past.

Miriel Lenore's spare, taut style, with its subtle voice rhythms,
carries the strength and precariousness of someone who asks
how she may begin to belong in the desert as her feet tell her
she does in Adelaide.

drums & bonnets
Miriel Lenore

In *drums & bonnets*, we follow Miriel Lenore's search for
clues to the life of her great-grandmother, Lizzie, on a poetic
pilgrimage that moves from the troubles of Northern Ireland to
the goldfields of Ballarat. She brings back tales from the past,
interwoven with fresh and incisive evocations of people, places
and dramatic situations.

These lucid and sensitive poems probe history and myth,
leaving and arriving, public and private, home, religion and
gold – all in the life of one unknown woman.

the Dog Rock
Miriel Lenore

Following the success of *drums & bonnets*, Miriel Lenore takes us on a new poetic journey to find her great-great-grandmother, Sarah. In *the Dog Rock* Sarah escapes with husband and children from the rural poverty and riots of the 1830s in Sussex to settle on the western slopes of the Dividing Range in New South Wales.

In this compelling volume, Lenore threads past with present, the social and political with the personal. Tragedy and quiet achievement underscore the complex effects of religion in the life of this first settler at Dog Rock where her family still live and farm. Once again, Lenore's sensitive vision, economy and strength of narrative continue to delight.

a wild kind of tune
Miriel Lenore

The title of this poetry narrative – *a wild kind of tune* – captures perfectly the imaginative journey into the poignant psycho-geography of Miriel Lenore's maternal great-grandmother, Caroline. In a wild tale arcing from 1845 to the present, in poetry underpinned by meticulous research, we inhabit settler society with all its attendant joys, hardship and grief as we careen with Caroline through her journey of love, loss and horror into madness.

The use of the actual medical records from late nineteenth century Asylums for the Insane (Gladesville and Kenmore) is chilling in the extreme; the rendering of these facts into a narrative of sensitive family history a partial redemption, a heartfelt honouring, of Caroline's bitter life. Lenore has made an important literary contribution to our understanding of the mistreatment of the mentally ill, especially women, in Australia's history.

Printed in Australia
AUHW010108030619
312937AU00004B/4

9 781743 056448